Magic of the Seasons

poems from the collection
of
Joan Esterline Lafuze

Joan Esterline Lafuze
November 12th, 2022

MAGIC OF THE SEASONS
First Printing
Copyright 2022 © Joan Esterline Lafuze

All rights reserved. No portion of this book may be reproduced mechanically, electronically, or by any other means, including photocopying, without permission of the publisher or author except in the case of brief quotations embodied in critical articles and reviews. It is illegal to copy this book, post it to a website, or distribute it by any other means without permission from the publisher or author.

Illustrations by Codie L. Kirby

ISBN -- 978-1-0880-4171-0 (hardcover)

ISBN -- 978-1-0879-7115-5 (paperback)

ISBN -- 978-1-0880-4159-8 (eBook)

The Lesson of the Scarlet Maple

Do not worry, the nurseryman said.
Its leaves will stay green through the summer heat
and autumn's cool days when other trees greet
us with foliage of gold and orange and red.

But this maple waits for the bitter cold
to display the brightest and best of all—
a burst of scarlet refusing to fall
when the others sigh and give up their hold.

We long to learn the lessons you teach,
Eternal Nurseryman. Safely keeping
the keys to understanding you employ,
you help us know how we must stretch to reach
beyond with ease. Through trial we learn that weeping
through the night brings a brilliant morning joy!

Dedication

Magic of the Seasons is dedicated to Mary Fell and Brian Brodeur in celebration of their support of creative writing and poetry at Indiana University East. In their honor, all book proceeds will go to the Indiana University Foundation's Maurene Specht Scholarship which supports the work of English students at Indiana University East.

Acknowledgements

I am grateful to Janice Wilkins for her ongoing and daily support of all my efforts and endeavors. I so appreciate the guidance of Denise Cassino in creating and compiling this book. I truly value the creative talents of Codie Kirby in making this book so very beautiful. They have all made it come to life in a magical way.

In addition, I would like to acknowledge the Tom Bird Organization.

Table of Contents

Foreword   11

Spring   19

Summer   27

Autumn   35

Winter   41

Christmas   51

New Year   95

About the Author   103

Foreword

Joan Lafuze is a dear friend. We belong to the same church, and it was at a church-sponsored poetry workshop that we learned that we both enjoy reading and writing poetry. I am flattered to have been asked to write the Foreward for *Magic of the Seasons*, and I'm thrilled to do it. That's because I love this woman and I love her poetry. Furthermore, I love the way she has lived her life.

Joan, more than anyone else I've known, uses both sides of her brain, right and left, creative and analytic. Just look at her professional title: Joan Esterline Lafuze, Ph.D. Professor of Biology Emerita. That alone tells you she's made good use of the science side of things. I might add that Joan acquired that Ph.D. years ago while simultaneously working as a wife and mother at home with her late husband Ralph and their three daughters and a son. That the son, Robert, had schizophrenia, added to Joan's motivation to learn, especially the biology of the brain.

This past year I watched Joan heroically fight, and win, an intense battle against Covid 19. I am convinced that the love of Ralph and their children resides in her very bones (science not withstanding) and has sustained her through the trials and hardships of her life. It is also the font from which flows the joy and wonder that brings forth the poet.

The poems she has collected, without exception, stimulate thought. They are literary pieces which have been important to Joan and are placed within these pages to share with the reader. They will serve the reader as they have served Joan, bringing comfort or insight as needed. They also serve to enhance those poems written by Joan, a kind of illustration if you will.

The poems she has written are simply beautiful to the ear and call for a second or third reading before moving on. Some tell a story. ("The Pink Magnolias at Saint Bridget 1998" is a good example.) Others recreate a time and scene remembered. (See "Ode to a Fallen Tree.") Still others just seem lovely to flow through one's mind while being heard by the ear ("Bloom, Baby, Bloom"). Be sure and read those aloud.

Joan's poems could come only from a person of great faith. Her Christmas card poems, written as gifts to family and friends during the lean early years of Ralph's law practice, are exactly that. Gifts. They bring not only joy and wonderment, but whimsy and delight as well.

I can't overstate the quality of these poems. Each is itself an actual poem by a talented poet. These poems will stand the test of time. They will be great decades, even generations, from now. They are simply well written poems. They do what poetry always does. They remind us of our place in God's universe. Her Christmas collection further reminds us of God's place in our lives. They express gratitude for what has been and what will be.

Gratitude is an important element in Joan's make-up. She is grateful for every day. For every person, place, and thing along the way. Furthermore, she expresses that gratitude. She is kind, gracious and generous. For years I referred to her as "The Rose Lady." That's because I watched her week after week, year after year (prior to the pandemic, of course) bring a huge colorful bouquet of roses to church each Sunday. At the end of the service, she would rise from her seat and would hand out those roses, one at a time, one to a person, as she made her way to the exit. I never saw a pattern as to who did and who did not receive a rose along her way. I only know I came to think of it as a kind of offering from her in addition to whatever financial gifts she gave. All I know for sure is that those roses contributed to the wellbeing of God's people. Every rose brought a smile. All the way to the parking lot and beyond.

The poems within these pages will solicit smiles, tears, remembrances, and curiosity. Some might evoke appreciation, while others might stimulate a change in course. Poetry does that. Good poems do it well. Those who designed these pages are to be commended. The reader will find beauty in not only the words but also in the lovely illustrations.

They are simple yet perfect for the page. Each is drawn exactly for the words it accompanies. Together, these poems and these drawings, are lovely. Just the right amount of art in a book is like just the right amount of salt in a sauce.

Enjoy.

Donna Monday

The Rose Lady
by Donna Monday

She is a mother,
A widow,
A professor,
A friend.

But on Sunday mornings
She is the rose lady.

She sits, with her family,
In a pew down front.

She sings,
She prays,
She listens.

And as the sermon ends and the benediction is said,
She stands,

Cradled in her arms is a huge bouquet of roses:
Reds, pinks, yellows--all colors.

She begins giving the roses away,
One by one.
Somehow, she knows who wants
Or needs a rose this day.

This Sunday I am a recipient,
And I am grateful.
Receiving a rose from the Rose Lady feels,
In some small way,
Like receiving communion.

I choose a pink one.
It spends the week--Sunday to Sunday
In a little vase on a ledge above my kitchen sink.

"You are loved," it whispers,
"You are forgiven."

The little rose in the little vase
Has fulfilled its ministry.

After the seas are all cross'd, (as they seem already cross'd,)
After the great captains and engineers have accomplish'd their work,
After the noble inventors, after the scientists, the chemist, the geologist, ethnologist,
Finally shall come the poet worthy that name,
The true son of God shall come singing his songs.

- Walt Whitman, *Leaves of Grass*

If, after reading any one of the poems in this volume you are willing to rethink preconceived notions or contemplate new, risky, imaginative ideas, I will be eternally grateful!

- Joan

Spring

Spring is a season of rebirth—
whether we think of it as life's coming into being this spring only or whether we think of it from a "perennial" perspective of annual rebirth. We "come to life" and are reborn to "bloom and blossom" once more.

- Joan

Spring
by Christina Rosetti

There is no time like Spring,
When life's alive in everything,
Before new nestlings sing,
Before cleft swallows speed their journey back
Along the trackless track, –
God guides their wing,
He spreads their table that they nothing lack, –
Before the daisy grows a common flower,
Before the sun has power
To scorch the world up in his noontide hour.

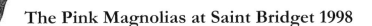

The Pink Magnolias at Saint Bridget 1998

The pink magnolias were the first to go
at Saint Bridget. Harbingers of spring,
they were more faithful than any bird could sing
to signal winter's end. The blend of soft pink buds
against burgundy brick whispered low,
"Come on in through this hidden back way
to the wonders of Indianapolis!"

It was mid-winter when the reaper struck
the heavy blow that quickly took them down.
One day skeletons danced against the bricks
as the wind made arms and legs bend and sway
to the upbeat of a maestro gone wild.
The magnolia trees soon disappeared.
Few of us remain to mourn their tragic end.

Is there an Eternal Soul who feels our
pain of loss and despair for what is gone?
Can there be One Who Remembers
our longing for a glimpse of beauty
or the touch of a loved-one who has gone ahead?
For the measure of beauty is not the time it lasts,
it is its quality instead.

Bloom, Baby, Bloom

We whisper
    A child
  Born to breathe
      Breathe, Baby, breathe
        Become our breath
Promise of tomorrow

We shout
    A child
  Born to bruise
      Break, Baby, break
        Burst our bonds
Free us from yesterday

We sing
    A child
  Born to bloom
      Bloom, Baby, bloom
        Bless our birth
Joy of today

Hold Us When We Hurt

GOD
HOLD US WHEN WE HURT!
Take us in your arms and calm our fears.
Fold us to your heart that we can catch its beat
    and set the rhythm of our lives.
Warm us with your tears
    and breathe encouragement as we grow wise.
        In wisdom
            born of pain.

TRUST US TO LOVE!
Tease its impulse from the morn of yesterday
    and free it to disturb us at this HOLY HOUR.
Turn us to the twilight of tomorrow
    with new purity and power.

                        BEHOLD US
                  RECREATED
                and
              REBORN!
      amen

Summer

June, July, and August are times of summer sun and lingering heat. We hear the lovely murmur of life and see it glistening in June. June leads to rising heat and the glow of humidity in July which finally gives way to its fullest height in August.

- Joan

Excerpt from *The Vision of Sir Launfal*
by James Russell Lowell

And what is so rare as a day in June?
    Then, if ever, come perfect days;
Then Heaven tries the earth if it be in tune,
    And over it softly her warm ear lays:
Whether we look, or whether we listen,
We hear life murmur, or see it glisten;

        * * *

That skies are clear, and grass is growing;
The breeze comes whispering in our ear,
That dandelions are blossoming near,
    That maize has sprouted, that streams are flowing,
That the river is bluer than the sky,
That the robin is plastering his house hard by;
And if the breeze kept the good news back,
For other couriers we should not lack;
    We could guess it all by yon heifer's lowing,—
And hark! how clear bold chanticleer,
Warmed with the new wine of the year,
Tells all in his lusty crowing!

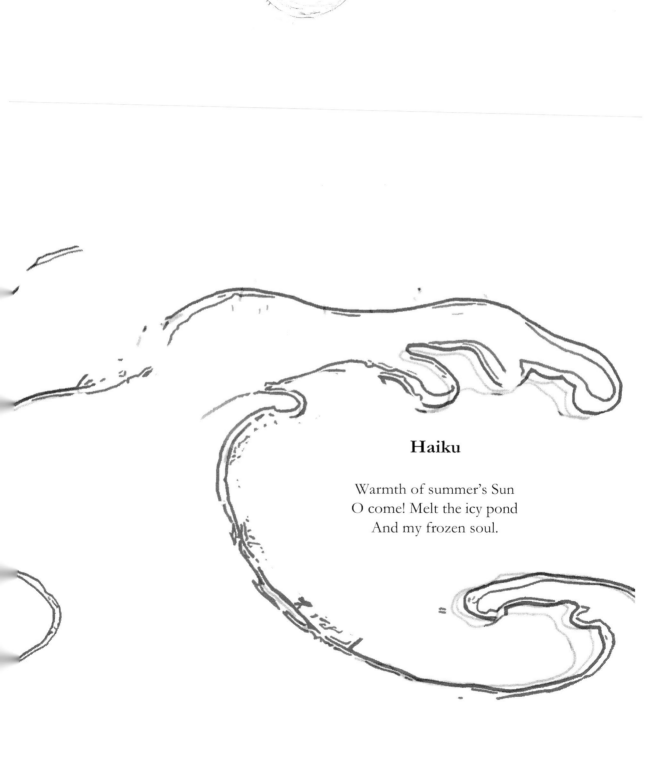

Haiku

Warmth of summer's Sun
O come! Melt the icy pond
And my frozen soul.

Treadmill

It was her glistening skin that first caught my eye.
Rich, deep brown gave hints of hidden gold.
Her long, left leg stretched forward to defy the bold
backward lurch of her shoulder on that side.

A second look reads history on her skin.
Scars mark her knees shouting the price she pays
to keep on moving but not ahead. She stays
in place. It is a race she cannot win.

Road of life, I wonder how long the pace
you set will match the strength I have to move.
I keep on going, but never change my place
in line. I stride and strive to keep above
the ordinary. Strength comes, and I face
this longer run on your road that I love.

Olive Tree

Ancient Tree, gnarled and wise, you teach that when beaten,
life thrives where roots run strong and deep.
Your root survives both fire then frost to keep
your hidden strength alive. You rise to bloom again!

Ancient Tree, gnarled and wise, your fruit feeds
our bodies. Its oil fills the lamp that lights our way.
Sacred oil anoints lesions of the day
and soothes the soul. It satisfies our needs.

Ancient Tree, you bridge the message of love
from long ago to meet the modern mind.
Your branch, your leaf, your little friend, the dove,
bring hope. They promise peace we long to find.
For life stops not, and ever on the move
it bothers neither to be gentle nor kind.

Autumn

How brief the time of Autumn, and how precious are those weeks between mid-September and All Saints Day! It is a time of emotions that are opposite in nature. Like misers, we treasure the crisp clean air and intensely blue skies. We mourn the disappearance of long days, and the sorrow of loss balances the beauty of the leaves of the scarlet maple trees.

- Joan

October's Bright Blue Weather
by Helen Hunt Jackson

When comrades seek sweet country haunts,
By twos and twos together,
And count like misers, hour by hour,
October's bright blue weather.

O suns and skies and flowers of June,
Count all your boasts together,
Love loveth best of all the year
October's bright blue weather.

Ode to a Fallen Tree

I found the tree that autumn day
lying low so it blocked my way
to no place certain. I sat down
to watch the birds and squirrels play.

Soft rain sprinkled its wild branched hair
which once tossed free—without a care
close to the clouds in a clear blue sky
flaunting life in the open air.

Soft rain washed my soul and face
and freed me to enjoy this space
without fear. I arose in peace
seeking paths to a brand-new place.

Oh Tree, did you descend from high
and Holy places just to tie
heaven to earth and reveal to me
a better path to travel by?

The Lesson of the Scarlet Maple

Do not worry, the nurseryman said.
Its leaves will stay green through the summer heat
and autumn's cool days when other trees greet
us with foliage of gold and orange and red.

But this maple waits for the bitter cold
to display the brightest and best of all—
a burst of scarlet refusing to fall
when the others sigh and give up their hold.

We long to learn the lessons you teach,
Eternal Nurseryman. Safely keeping
the keys to understanding you employ,
you help us know how we must stretch to reach
beyond with ease. Through trial we learn that weeping
through the night brings a brilliant morning joy!

Winter

Winter enters with freezing winds and blowing snow all about. That snow covers everything in its path making familiar objects seem unclear! Winter days are shorter and make a stranger of the hiding sun. Often life seems hopeless until Albert Camus reminds us of the invincible summer bringing hope once again.

- Joan

"In the midst of winter, I found there was, within me, an invincible summer."

- Albert Camus

The Snowstorm
by Ralph Waldo Emerson

Announced by all the trumpets of the sky,
Arrives the snow, and, driving o'er the fields,
Seems nowhere to alight: the whited air
Hides hills and woods, the river, and the heaven,
And veils the farm-house at the garden's end.

When Winter Comes

When winter comes, who dares to dream of spring?
Who opens up to catch the bitter air
and fails to dodge ice bullets everywhere
hitting the tender places with their sting?
It is no time to prod the voice to sing
of better times that dared to disappear
or worse ones that echo their despair.
What kind of song can this December bring?

Uncommon Bond

Too soon we brace to meet bold winter's sting.
Offended by the rude December wind
    we are stunned by its mocking whistling
    and its bitter cold. We search for you, our friend.
How well we remember your comforting
    ways. You heard us and hastened to defend
    against icy fears and the overwhelming
    pain of loss and of grieving without end.

Love generates the warmest, brightest light
    of all in the deep, dark December night.
Love transcends human bounds of wrong and right
    and shines on all our paths to make them bright.

Winter Wisdom

Haunted, failed, lost in December we chose
points of faith frozen in the onyx night
to follow—just the right amount of light
when darkness hides the way and memory slows.

Fixed in place by the same cold wind that blows,
the pond reflects the sun's rays, full and bright,
in morning, making the bleak evening light
and bearing the weight of heavy winter snows.

Spring love frolics, but always with the fear
of loss. Never quite certain it can hold
on tight enough, it is not free to live.

Winter love lets go. No doubt it will bear
our full weight keeps us from becoming bold.
We are free—not to take, but free to give.

Song of Sorrow

Look at me and feel my sorrow.

See my head bowed and sense my pain.

Pray for me. Each day I borrow

strength to face life in peace again.

Christmas

The following poems are selected from a Christmas card collection that Ralph and I began when he was starting his law practice in Richmond, and we had no other gifts to give our families and closest friends. We continued the tradition for over fifty years even after his practice flourished. The list of recipients grew also. I wrote the poems, and for the first year, I handmade the cards. After that year, Ralph arranged to have them printed.

Ralph's favorite poet was Ogden Nash. He quoted Ogden frequently and introduced me to Professor Twist, the conscientious scientist. He "pretended" not to understand the kind of poetry I wrote. We laughed when he told me one year, "My God, something must have gone wrong. I almost understand this one."

```
           O
          FIR
         TEACH
         US WELL
        THAT LIFE
       REMAINS WHILE
      OTHER SIGNS ARE
      HIDDEN STAND AND
     REACH TOWARD HEAVEN
     AS IF TO TELL   A STAR
     WILL LEAD TO HOPE, LOVE
           A
           N
           D
       LIFE ABUNDANT
```

```
                O
               FIR
              TEACH
             US WELL
            THAT LIFE
          REMAINS WHILE
         OTHER SIGNS ARE
        HIDDEN. STAND AND
       REACH TOWARD HEAVEN
      AS  IF  TO  TELL  .  A  STAR
     WILL  LEAD  TO  HOPE,  LOVE
                A
                N
                D
          LIFE  ABUNDANT
```

Hope is Born

An angel sings this Holy Night

When Love slips in and seals the darkness

Where Faith works best.

It is this very night that Hope is born and leaves at dawn
to live and die and fall beneath the Sun.

You know the rest. That is, you know the rest
except perhaps the answer to this question:

Why would angels sing at such a birth?

Why would angels sing for one who as a man spoke simple
words of seeds and trees and sons and other common things
that grow and live and die and fall beneath the sun to bloom
again at night when Love slips in and Faith works best?

A mystery we say—it is a miracle when angels sing before the morn.

And so we miss the meaning, night by night when in silence.
Love seals the darkness tight and makes a place where Hope is born.

```
                O
               FIR
              TEACH
             US WELL
            THAT LIFE
          REMAINS WHILE
         OTHER SIGNS ARE
         HIDDEN. STAND AND
        REACH TOWARD HEAVEN
       AS  IF  TO  TELL  -  A  STAR
      WILL  LEAD  TO  HOPE,  LOVE
                A
                N
                D
           LIFE ABUNDANT
```

Christmas Child

Become a child this Christmas.
Laugh aloud with glee
at the tinsel, ball, and bow
and popcorn on the tree.

Become a child this Christmas.
Wonder at the light
and warmth of candle burning
at the twinkling bright
array of star-glow, turning
us away from night.

Sing a song this Christmas.
Be an angel unaware.
Bring the joy of heaven
to a life which needs you there.

Become a child this Christmas
in a way that is filled
with God, who made and loved us,
and became a Child.

```
           O
          FIR
         TEACH
        US WELL
       THAT LIFE
     REMAINS WHILE
    OTHER SIGNS ARE
   HIDDEN. STAND AND
  REACH TOWARD HEAVEN
 AS IF TO TELL - A STAR
WILL LEAD TO HOPE, LOVE
           A
           N
           D
      LIFE ABUNDANT
```

All is Found

Trees are bare
    Leaves lie on the ground
        All is lost

All is found

Birds have flown
    No music fills the air
        All is lost

All is found

Sun has set
    Light and warmth are gone
        All is lost

All is found

Love is lost
    We've searched everywhere
        All is lost

All is found

                In the Orient
                A Babe is Born
                Who finds a cross
                All is lost

All is found

```
             O
            FIR
           TEACH
          US WELL
         THAT LIFE
       REMAINS WHILE
       OTHER SIGNS ARE
       HIDDEN. STAND AND
      REACH TOWARD HEAVEN
     AS IF TO TELL   A STAR
    WILL  LEAD  TO  HOPE,  LOVE
             A
             N
             D
         LIFE ABUNDANT
```

Second Wind

Spirit

Conception   Confusion   Christmas
Cradle   Cross   Crown
Consecration   Chaos   Coronation
Maiden Mother
Infant Son
Nations
Born in God
Who know His Name
For all who walk from night
Yea, run toward morn
The pattern and the promise are the same

They shall endure who
Breathe pure air and
Catch new life

Second Wind
Come in
Dwell
Swell
In
Us
A
M
E
N

```
            O
           FIR
          TEACH
         US WELL
        THAT LIFE
      REMAINS WHILE
     OTHER SIGNS ARE
    HIDDEN. STAND AND
   REACH TOWARD HEAVEN
  AS  IF  TO  TELL  ·  A  STAR
 WILL  LEAD  TO  HOPE,  LOVE
            A
            N
            D
      LIFE  ABUNDANT
```

Today is Christmas

Today

is

Christmas

Can You Hear

God

Sing A Birthday

Song?

Yesterday And Tomorrow

Belong In Harmony

Today Is Melody

Melody Rings Clear

Christmas

is

Today

```
                O
               FIR
              TEACH
             US WELL
            THAT LIFE
          REMAINS WHILE
         OTHER SIGNS ARE
        HIDDEN. STAND AND
       REACH TOWARD HEAVEN
      AS IF TO TELL - A STAR
     WILL LEAD TO HOPE, LOVE
                A
                N
                D
           LIFE ABUNDANT
```

Peace on Earth

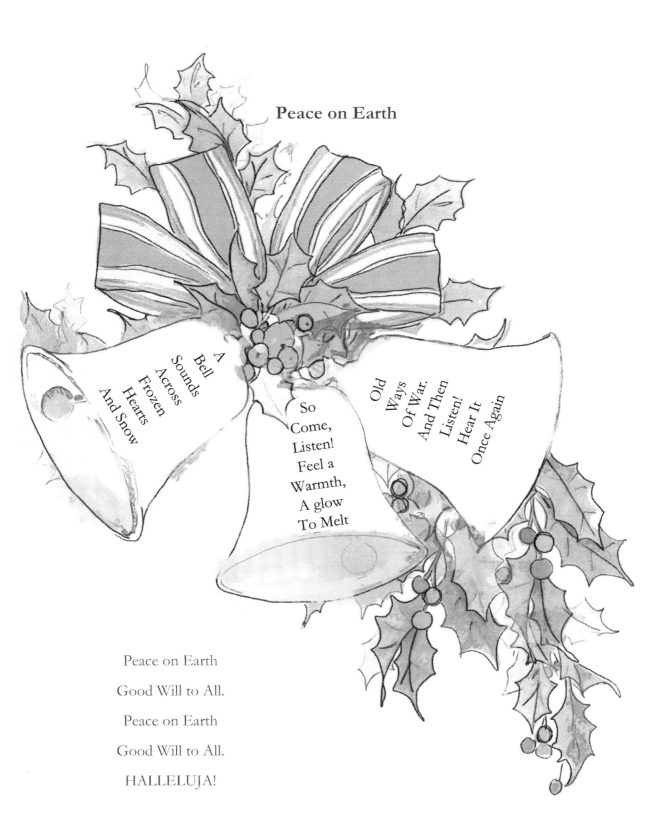

A Bell Sounds Across Frozen Hearts And Snow

So Come, Listen! Feel a Warmth, A glow To Melt

Old Ways Of War. And Then Listen! Hear It Once Again

Peace on Earth

Good Will to All.

Peace on Earth

Good Will to All.

HALLELUJA!

```
            O
           FIR
          TEACH
         US WELL
        THAT LIFE
      REMAINS WHILE
     OTHER SIGNS ARE
    HIDDEN. STAND AND
   REACH TOWARD HEAVEN
  AS  IF  TO  TELL   A STAR
 WILL  LEAD  TO  HOPE,  LOVE
            A
            N
            D
       LIFE ABUNDANT
```

Christmas Sonnet

Midwinter memories linger with the fun
of youth. Energy matched the burst of Spring.
Our voices rolled to Heaven and the ring
carried (we were certain) to the Sun.

Tell us now. Spring is over, Summer gone,
and Autumn passed. What joy can Christmas bring
to us? Our muted voices cannot sing.
What lasts? All we loved has gone—one by one.

Lo! Christmas enters—chill December. Snow
and ice succumb to spring winds warm and mild.
Heaven's voices ring and sing for us below
the melodies of gladness. Our hearts, beguiled
by the magic of brand new life, will know
the best is yet to come. Behold a Child!

```
                O
               FIR
              TEACH
             US WELL
            THAT LIFE
          REMAINS WHILE
         OTHER SIGNS ARE
        HIDDEN. STAND AND
       REACH TOWARD HEAVEN
      AS IF TO TELL   A STAR
     WILL LEAD TO HOPE, LOVE
               A
               N
               D
          LIFE ABUNDANT
```

At Christmas

At Christmas
    one beholds
    a robe of joy
    with sorrow
    in its folds.

At Christmas
    one follows
    a star of light
    with sadness
    in its shadows.

At Christmas
    one must bring
    a servant gifts
    intended
    for a king.

    God takes one's
    intentions
    and expands life
    to new dimensions
At Christmas.

```
              O
             FIR
            TEACH
           US WELL
          THAT LIFE
        REMAINS WHILE
       OTHER SIGNS ARE
      HIDDEN. STAND AND
     REACH TOWARD HEAVEN
    AS  IF  TO  TELL  -  A  STAR
   WILL  LEAD  TO  HOPE,  LOVE
              A
              N
              D
        LIFE  ABUNDANT
```

For Heaven's Sake!

Can Christmas Make Sense?

A baby's birth . . .

For Heaven's sake!

How on Earth

Could it make

Any difference?

```
            O
           FIR
          TEACH
         US WELL
        THAT LIFE
      REMAINS WHILE
     OTHER SIGNS ARE
    HIDDEN. STAND AND
   REACH TOWARD HEAVEN
  AS  IF  TO  TELL  -  A STAR
 WILL  LEAD  TO  HOPE,  LOVE
           A
           N
           D
      LIFE ABUNDANT
```

The Christmas Rose

The span is marked from eve to eve,
    is measured off in holy hours
        so some assert
        and perch alert
    in dreamy distant towers.
They search a sign to force belief.

The span is marked through highs and lows
    from life to life in constant flow
        so some believe
        and dare to live
    walking out across the snow.
They stoop to pluck the Christmas rose.

```
              O
             FIR
            TEACH
           US WELL
          THAT LIFE
        REMAINS WHILE
        OTHER SIGNS ARE
        HIDDEN. STAND AND
       REACH TOWARD HEAVEN
       AS IF TO TELL - A STAR
      WILL LEAD TO HOPE, LOVE
              A
              N
              D
          LIFE ABUNDANT
```

Baby Boy

Christmas

is a love to share,

Christmas

is a birthday joy,

Christmas

is a mother's prayer,

Christmas

is a Baby Boy.

```
            O
           FIR
          TEACH
         US WELL
        THAT LIFE
      REMAINS WHILE
     OTHER SIGNS ARE
    HIDDEN. STAND AND
   REACH TOWARD HEAVEN
  AS IF TO TELL   A STAR
 WILL LEAD TO HOPE, LOVE
           A
           N
           D
      LIFE ABUNDANT
```

Promised Child

Amid the shouts of wrong and right

and clash of arms—ensuing fight

    the human ear

        to din and roar inured

    still strains to catch

        the Whispered Word.

Weighted by the wicked fright

of snow and cold and starless night

    the human heart

        by dread and fear set wild

    now calms to await

        a Promised Child.

```
                O
               FIR
              TEACH
             US WELL
            THAT LIFE
          REMAINS WHILE
         OTHER SIGNS ARE
        HIDDEN. STAND AND
      REACH TOWARD HEAVEN
     AS IF TO TELL   A STAR
    WILL  LEAD  TO  HOPE,  LOVE
               A
               N
               D
          LIFE ABUNDANT
```

Betrayal

Our Christmas thought this year was *all's well that ends*.
The losses are too great to bear. The fear
of sleep evokes wild day mares that bring sheer
terror before the lonely night descends.

Where is our passion for true peace, Dear Friends?
Or when will we speak through love-acts with clear,
pure voices? What pathway will bring us near
the answers upon which our being whole depends?

God, we asked you to teach us how to love
one another. We begged you for help to mend
our warring ways on an earth we have defiled.
We beseeched you to give us power to move
the world to a peace we trusted you to send.
And all you sent us was a little child.

```
              O
             FIR
            TEACH
           US WELL
          THAT LIFE
        REMAINS WHILE
       OTHER SIGNS ARE
      HIDDEN. STAND AND
     REACH TOWARD HEAVEN
    AS IF TO TELL - A STAR
   WILL LEAD TO HOPE, LOVE
             A
             N
             D
       LIFE ABUNDANT
```

God Wise

Only fools leave power and pride behind
in order to chase a star!
An outrageous price
to pay for so little.
What could they hope to find?
Is it to mock we call them wise?

Offer them no pity
for they have no place
to put it
Since once upon a
night they knelt
in awe
before a babe and felt
the power of newborn purity.

The rule of uncommon sense applies:
They are world foolish but God-wise.

```
          O
         FIR
        TEACH
        US WELL
       THAT LIFE
      REMAINS WHILE
     OTHER SIGNS ARE
    HIDDEN. STAND AND
   REACH TOWARD HEAVEN
  AS  IF  TO  TELL  -  A STAR
 WILL  LEAD  TO  HOPE,  LOVE
           A
           N
           D
      LIFE ABUNDANT
```

Home of Joy

The marble palace of happiness?
Take this broad highway bright.
Eagerly we snatched the map,
and followed every sign just right.
But by the map betrayed,
we felt cold fear annoy.
We saw the highway narrow
to a path more dimly lit by far.
Darkness forced us to look up
to a flick of light—a star!
And we stumbled on a stable—home of joy.

```
                O
               FIR
              TEACH
             US WELL
            THAT LIFE
          REMAINS WHILE
         OTHER SIGNS ARE
        HIDDEN. STAND AND
       REACH TOWARD HEAVEN
      AS IF TO TELL - A STAR
     WILL LEAD TO HOPE, LOVE
               A
               N
               D
         LIFE ABUNDANT
```

And Call It Christmas

LOVE

IGNITE
      the skies
              with flame

DANCE
      to light
           a child
                who coos and cries
                      into the night

HEAR
      the echo of lament

SENSE
      the silence of content
               (or is it frozen fear?)

HOLD
      us
        blind and deaf and lame

KEEP
      us
        mute
            until your flame
                      melts
                          from inside out

FREE
    tear
        to
           flow   heart
                    to
                        glow   hope
                                    to
                                      grow

MOVE
      limb
        to
          leap
                and
                    voice
                        to
                          shout
                                  YOUR
                                      NAME

AND CALL IT CHRISTMAS

```
            O
           FIR
          TEACH
         US WELL
        THAT LIFE
      REMAINS WHILE
     OTHER SIGNS ARE
    HIDDEN. STAND AND
   REACH TOWARD HEAVEN
   AS IF TO TELL - A STAR
  WILL LEAD TO HOPE, LOVE
            A
            N
            D
       LIFE ABUNDANT
```

God's Light

O
COME
WITH
US &
FIND
LOVE
IN A
BABY
JOY!
IN A
STAR
AND
TRUTH IN GOD'S
LIGHT!

```
                O
               FIR
              TEACH
             US WELL
            THAT LIFE
          REMAINS WHILE
         OTHER SIGNS ARE
        HIDDEN. STAND AND
       REACH TOWARD HEAVEN
      AS  IF  TO  TELL  -  A  STAR
     WILL  LEAD  TO  HOPE,  LOVE
                A
                N
                D
          LIFE  ABUNDANT
```

Christmas Tree

O

FIR

TEACH

US WELL

THAT LIFE

REMAINS WHILE

OTHER SIGNS ARE

HIDDEN. STAND AND

REACH TOWARD HEAVEN

AS IF TO TELL - A STAR

WILL LEAD TO HOPE, LOVE

A

N

D

LIFE ABUNDANT

```
                O
               FIR
              TEACH
             US WELL
            THAT LIFE
          REMAINS WHILE
         OTHER SIGNS ARE
        HIDDEN. STAND AND
       REACH TOWARD HEAVEN
      AS IF TO TELL  -  A STAR
    WILL  LEAD  TO  HOPE,  LOVE
               A
               N
               D
          LIFE ABUNDANT
```

Justified by Faith

We embrace December and welcome the sheer
bright nights that lead to daytime's crunchy snow—
a white blanket that gives mistakes the glow
of lessons learned. Forgiveness is made clear!

We embrace December—an end to this year
and a gate to the next, where we will go
with memory of what we need to know
to live with understanding and not fear.

God, signal with the ringing of your bells
and flinging in the night so bright a star
that when we reach and touch as faith compels,
we see our lives right justified from far
on high—not by what we manage for ourselves,
but through Your power, Your grace and who You are!

```
             O
            FIR
           TEACH
           US WELL
          THAT LIFE
        REMAINS WHILE
       OTHER SIGNS ARE
      HIDDEN. STAND AND
     REACH TOWARD HEAVEN
   AS  IF  TO  TELL     A  STAR
  WILL  LEAD  TO  HOPE,  LOVE
            A
            N
            D
      LIFE ABUNDANT
```

God Reaches Down

God sends His Life
> from highest heaven
> to lowest earth
> to bridge the rift.

The miracle of Christmas time?
God reaches down—presents His Gift.

No worthy match
> but best we have
> to Him in Heaven
> our lives we lift.

The miracle of Christmas time?
God reaches down—accepts our gift.

```
               O
              FIR
             TEACH
            US WELL
           THAT LIFE
         REMAINS WHILE
         OTHER SIGNS ARE
        HIDDEN. STAND AND
        REACH TOWARD HEAVEN
       AS IF TO TELL - A STAR
       WILL LEAD TO HOPE, LOVE
               A
               N
               D
          LIFE ABUNDANT
```

God, Teach Us to Be Holy

GOD
TEACH US TO BE HOLY
HELP US COUNT THE WINTER CANDLES ONE BY ONE

UNTIL WE'VE CAUGHT THE WARMTH AND LIGHT
TO LAST 'TIL SPRING USHERS IN THE SUMMER SUN

HELP US SING THE HOLY SONG AND SEND IT OUT
ACROSS THE SNOW

TO CATCH THE EAR OF ONE WHO STANDS
ALONE OUTSIDE A DOOR
AND HAS NO HOME

GOD
TEACH US TO BE HOLY
HELP US COUNT THE WINTER CANDLES ONE BY ONE

UNTIL WE LEARN THE SONGS THE HOMELESS SING
AND THROUGH THEM
UNDERSTAND YOUR TRUTH

BUT FOR TONIGHT
LET THE HEAVENS RING WITH JOY
AS TOGETHER WE HOLD HANDS AND WAIT FOR DAWN.

GOD
TEACH US TO BE HOLY
HELP US COUNT THE WINTER CANDLES ONE BY ONE

WHATEVER LIFE BESTOWS OR KEEPS
THERE IS NO CHRISTMAS JOY DENIED US
BECAUSE EMANUEL COMES WE KNOW
GOD WEEPS
GOD LOVES
GOD WALKS BESIDE US

New Year

Eternal God, teach us to embrace the possible happiness

that each new year can bring.

Epiphany

Lost somewhere between here and there, we go
from place to place concerned that nothing makes
any sense at all. Both lost and found, terror shakes
us in our confidence. We wander to and fro.
Where are answers when we don't even know
the true questions? We trust the power that takes
wee wisps of frozen white and fashions flakes,
which weave a path. We trudge across the snow.

Love teaches us to trust the unseen way,
which opens just when darkness breaks to dawn,
revealing a small cradle where God lay.
Then we are filled with strength to carry on.
Our spirits lift while watching snowflakes play.
It takes so little light to lead us home.

Journey To A New Year

We traveled back to find the very site
that we last knew right where we were going.
The path was gone—hidden by the blowing
snow. We trudged ahead hardly knowing
where to step next in the dark winter night.
Then morning came with its brief brilliant light,
and diamond sunrays reflected—showing
us a path—a different way of going
home to warmth, love and laughter's sheer delight.

We welcome winter with new paths to trace
across the snow until one leads us near
to newborn joy. Never will we replace
treasured memories, but look to the clear
bright sun with arms open to embrace
the happiness ahead in this New Year.

The Way Home

December wends its way by candlelight.
Gone is the young, capricious step of Spring.
In Summer's stride there is no lingering
toward Autumn's bold walk to seek the night.

December fills with faith that the lamp's bright
flame will last long enough for us to bring
gifts of pure love, faith that peace bells will ring
and angel song will woo the wrong to right.

When boundaries are blurred by falling snow,
we cannot find the path that sets us free.
We only know the way that we have come.

Oh, Keeper of the Seasons, help us see,
even if by flickering candle glow,
the path to take from Bethlehem to home.

About the Author

IU East photo

I have always loved poetry. My mother read poetry to us as children, and I remember being captivated by the rhyme and rhythm that was in style then. I love rhyme and meter. Both provide the freedom of boundaries. In an essay that my son wrote in the sixth grade, his primary focus was how much he loved being free, but he captured the necessity of boundaries by writing, "but freedom can be like a severed artery."

All of my children inherited my love of poetry. My youngest child, Mary, has a special gift for writing poetry. When she was in the second grade, her teacher told my husband Ralph and me that she wrote her assignments in rhyme.

Although I continued my love of poetry and language, I chose a career in science. Eventually I became a systems medical physiologist and as such took a position in the Department of Biology at Indiana University East (IU East). While there, I had the opportunity to learn the "academic" side of poetry and was able to take two classes taught by "resident poets, Mary Fell and Brian Brodeur." I thank Mary for her inspiration and her ability to breathe encouragement. I thank Brian for teaching me the "basics" of poetry such as elegy, ode, narrative poetry and free verse. I was already fully aware of my favorite genre, the sonnet, that provides the freedom of rhyme, meter and structure.

Joan Esterline Lafuze

Made in the USA
Middletown, DE
07 October 2022